LA ALPUJARRA

Text by: José Manuel Real Pascual

Photographs, diagrams and reproduction
entirely conceived and produced by
EDITORIAL ESCUDO DE ORO S.A.

Copyright of this edition on photographs and literary text:
© EDITORIAL ESCUDO DE ORO S.A.
Palaudàries, 26 - 08004 Barcelona (Spain).

www.eoro.com
e-mail: editorial@eoro.com

DISTRIBUTOR: L. DOMINGUEZ, S.A.
Magallanes, 38 - Tel. 914 478 275
e-mail: ldominguez@ctv.es
28015 MADRID

Overall view of Bubión.

THE ALPUJARRA

The Alpujarra is one of Spain's most markedly personal districts. Over the past few years tourism has boomed there. The beauty, strength and contrasts of the land (the latter due above all to the sharp changes in altitude, dropping from the Mulhacén to the Costa del Sol in only 50 km), the layout of its towns and villages, the friendliness of its people, together with an historic past harking back to the Moslems, make this region one of Spain's most rewarding and interesting from the tourist point of view. Other factors add further to this interest: food and drink, the traditional festivities (above all the *romerías* to the mountains and the Moors and Christians festivities), and a climate of contrasts which allow both winter and summer sports to be practised.

The origins of the name of Alpujarra are a matter of some debate. One theory derives it from the first Moslem settler of the place, "Albujarra". However, many philologists see it as coming from the phrase "alba sierra" ('white mountains'). There is a mistaken opinion that the names of some of the towns and villages and other spots come from the Galician language. This idea appeared because there was an important colonisation of peasants of that part of Spain once the Moors had been expelled; this notwithstanding, as will be shown later, the original names predate this period.

The most important geographical feature

is the Sierra Nevada (literally 'Snowy Mountains'), the region's northern border. This mountain-range was also sometime known as *Orospeda, Solaria* or *Solair*. The Sierra Nevada is incomparable from the geographical and climatic point of view, and a view of it may be enjoyed from the many parts of the Alpujarra. There are several important peaks, the most outstanding being the Mulhacén, the highest mountain in the Iberian Peninsula, opposite which stands the village of Trevélez; another imposing peak is the Veleta, up to which lead Pampaneira, Bubión and Capileira. Of the several writers who have devoted their pens to this region, special mention must be made of two. The first is the British Hispanist Gerald Brenan, who immortalised the locality of Yegen. In order to get to known this region, its development and meaning, the reading of "South from Granada" is essential; this book was written between 1920 and 1930 in the house which the writer had in the village of Yegen. The second author deserving mention is Pedro Antonio de Alarcón, a writer from Guadix who, fifty years before, travelled through the district, producing a tome entitled "The Alpujarra". Both authors' works have been extensively consulted in the making of this guide.

Something that makes a great impression on all visitors to this district is the architecture of its villages, above all those standing in the Poqueira Ravine. Their streets are narrow and twisting, steep and designed for snowfalls, with the privatisation of public space being their hallmark. Roofs here are flat, built with stone slabs laid horizontally, in turn covered with shards of slate to protect against the rain. During the autumn and winter months, corn

Sierra Nevada.

A typical corner in Pampaneira.

Typical grille of Pampaneira. ▷

cobs and strings of peppers may be seen lying on these flat roofs or "terraos" as they are known locally. Other features worth mentioning are the "tinaos" or private terraces full of flowers, the most famous ones being those of Pampaneira. Another original aspect of the architecture of these villages are the chimneys; they are circular in shape and have to work for most of the year. One feature of note in the Alpujarra is craftsmanship, which may be considered a clear inheritor of its Christian Moor forebear. The most important artisan craft, and that with the longest tradition, is weaving. Over the past few years numerous craft shops have been established in the district which, in addition to the weaving looms, have relaunched the pottery and precious metal industries. Thanks to

this numerous artists and artisans have chosen the Alpujarra as their place of residence.

The Alpujarra's Arab past may be seen not only in its crafts, but also in customs, festivals and food and drink. In addition to this there are names of villages, natural and administrative areas, such as the "taha", a sort of municipal area still frequently used in such places as Pitres, otherwise known as "La Taha".

The number of hotel beds available has increased. There are hotels, hostals, guest houses and inns. The *casa de labranza* or country cottage hails from this area, and is hired out to groups of travellers. Campsites have also been established here, more specifically in Pitres and Trevélez, as well as a tourist village in Bubión.

The river Trevélez.

Typical street in Pampaneira.

Access routes

The national highway N-323 leading to Granada begins on the Costa del Sol, between Salobreña and Motril, 100 km from Málaga and 115 from Almería. From this road two access routes lead off. Along the first, 15 km from the coast, via Vélez de Benaudalla, and along the Umbría road, one reaches Orgiva 14 km later. The second access road, 29 km from the coast and 40 from Granada, leads to Orgiva after passing through the Tablate Bridge and Lanjarón, 15 km later. There is an eastern entry point to the Alpujarra from Guadix, crossing the mountain pass of La Ragua. It is also accessible from the coast via La Rábita and Adra. Finally, from Granada, after passing through the Sierra Nevada ski resort, one reaches Capileira, a route which is only practicable in summer.

In addition to being an introduction to the area, this guide also has sections on geography, history and food and drink. The core comprises a proposed route or itinerary, confined almost totally to the Upper and Western Alpujarra, with information of interest concerning the towns, villages and districts visited. This itinerary starts and ends at Orgiva, which could be regarded as being the capital of Western Alpujarra. Distances to the previous locality are provided in each of the places visited.

GEOGRAPHY

The Alpujarra is bounded to the north by the Sierra Nevada. The highest peak here

Overall view of Trevélez.

11,130 ft

is the Mulhacén (3,478 m); it is also the highest peak in the Iberian Peninsula. This is followed by the Veleta. The westernmost boundary is the Lecrín Valley. To the east there is a line linking the Sierra Nevada, the Sierra de Gádor and the delta of the river Andarax. To the south the Mediterranean coast may be considered as the natural boundary of this district. All of this lies within the provinces of Granada and Almería. It forms a depression between the Sierra Nevada and the more southerly ranges of Lújar, Contraviesa and Gádor; this depression contains the rivers Guadalfeo, Adra and Andarax, with their numerous tributaries such as the Poqueira, Trevélez and Mecina.

Over a distance of 50 km there is a drop of some 3,000 m in altitude towards the sea, with corresponding changes in climate and vegetation, as well as numerous advantages from the tourist point of view: the ski-slopes of Sierra Nevada and the warm waters of the Costa del Sol are only one hour from each other. The changes in temperature between summer and winter are very marked, as are the changes in humidity between the western and eastern areas.

The district's total surface area is 1,880 km². It includes 48 municipalities, 8 of which belong to Almería.

Farming is carried out on irrigated terraces, the main crops being cereals, beans, potatoes, chestnuts and cherries in the Upper Alpujarra. Olives oranges and vineyards in the Middle Alpujarra. Vines, almonds and figs in the Lower Alpujarra of the coastal area, together with substantial plantations of tropical fruits such as avocado pears, soursops, bananas and so on.

The Sierra Nevada offers a wide range of species in its flora, most of them alpine, which are only to be found here. Noteworthy are the mountain camomile and the Mulhacén poppy.

The population of the Alpujarra, after the blow of the expulsions of the Morisco population in 1492, 1570 and 1610, has grown only slowly due to emigration. Tourism may be one of the reasons preventing mass emigration nowadays from the area to the big cities. Figures given in the guide to the itinerary are rounded off since they change rapidly; they are useful only as a rough guide to the size of the different localities we are about to visit on the proposed route.

HISTORY

The history of the Alpujarra reached its high-water mark under the Arabs, and later in the 16th century when the Moriscos (Moslems converted to Christianity) revolted against the Christian troops of Philip II. Other parts of the area's history are not essential for a full appreciation of it, but nonetheless a description will be given of certain periods from prehistory to the present day.

Prehistory. The oldest human remains found in the Alpujarra go back to the Mesolithic period. Round about the fourth millenium BC the Neolithic age began in this part of the country; remains of this period have been found in the Bats' Cave near Albuñol, some 10 km from the Granada coast.

Arab castle in Lecrín.

SIERRA

Laguna La Mosca

Laguna Hondera

Laguna del
Peñon Negro

Río Dílar

Río Trevélez

Sierra

Aguadero

Río Dúrcal

Marchena

Cozvijar

El Puente

Río Torrente

SO-5

Dúrcal

Nigüetas

Cónchar

Acequias

SO-1

Lecrín

Melegís

Murchas

Mondújar

Saleres

Restabal

Chite

Béznar

Tablate

GR-120

Pinos del Valle

Izbor

Acebuches

Las Barreras

GR-130

Guájar-Alto

Guájar-Faragüit

SO-13

Guájar-Fondón

SO-18

Río de la Toba

Molvízar

SO-22

Lobres

Monte Almendras

Salobreña

El Varadero

Playa de la Charca

Playa de Poniente

Playa de las Azucenas

Torrenueva

Carchuna

Playa de Carchuna

Calahonda

Río Lanjarón

Río Chico

Lanjarón

Cáñar

Soportújar

Carataunas

Bayacas

Las Cañadillas

Cerro Negro

Agustines y Tijola

Orgiva

Los Tablones

Pago y
Benisalte

A-346

Embalse
de Rules

N-323

Vélez de Benaudalla

SE-21

La Gorgoracha

Lagos

Los Tablones

Motril

SE-28

SE-15

Gualchos

Los Pastores

Cuevas de Salas

La Garnatilla

Jolucar

Barranco del Hornillo

Los Carlos

La Torrera

Los García

Espinar Alto

Rambla del Agua

Barranco del Negro

Río Poqueira

Los Caballeros

GR-421

Capileira

Pampaneira

Bubión

Capilerilla

Pórtugos

Pitres

Mecina Fondales

Busquístar

Ferriola

La Solana

La Umbría

A-348

Los Románes

Alcázar

SE-02

Los Gallegos

Fregenite

Bargis

Haza del Lino

Olías

SE-42

Rubite

Polopos

SE-26

SE-41

Lújar

Las Casillas

Los Galvez

Los Barriales

Barranco Ferrer

Los Díaz

Haza del Trigo

SE-38

La Mamola

Trevélez

Fuentezuelas

Los Llanos

Castaras

Notaez

La Solana

Almegíjar

Cuesta de
Almendros

Torvizcón

La Umbría

GR-443

Los Salados

Los Morenos

Los Vargas

A-345

Alformón

El Maurel

Sorvilán

Los Caulines

SE-45

SE-4

Albondón

Los Galvez

Los Camillos

Albuñol

El Capitán

El Cortijo Bajo

El Haza Larga

Melicena

N-340

Los Yesos

La Mamola

Castillo de Baños

Castell de Ferro

Berchules

Alcutar

Juviles

Narila

Nieles

Timar

Lobres

Río Guadalfeo

Alba

Cuesta del Larg

Los C

Los Hue

La Err

El Acel

La Balsi

El Saltadero

La Ra

MAR

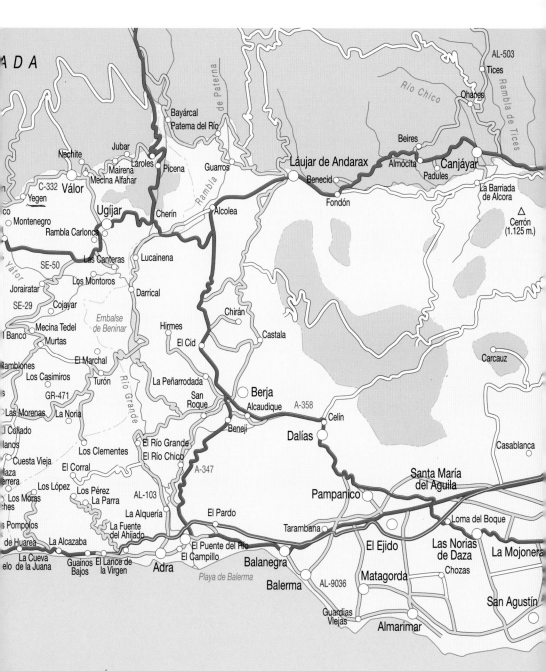

GRANADA

AL-503
Tices

Río Chico
Ohanes

Rambla de Tices

Bayárcal
Paterna del Río

Beires

Jubar
Nechite
Láujar de Andarax
Almócita
Padules
Canjáyar

Lároles
Mairena
Mecina Alfahar
Picena
Guarros
Benecid

C-332 Válor
Yegen
Fondón
La Barriada
de Alcora

Montenegro
Ugíjar
Cherín
Alcolea
Cerrón
(1.125 m.)

Rambla Carlonca
Rambla
de Paterna

SE-50
Las Canteras
Lucainena

Joráiratar
Los Montoros

SE-29
Cojáyar
Darrical

Embalse
de Beninar
Chirán

Mecina Tedel
Hirmes
Castala

Banco
Murtas
El Cid

Ramblones
El Marchal
Carcauz

Los Casimiros
Turón
La Peñarrodada

GR-471
Río Grande
San
Roque
Berja
A-358

Las Morenas
La Noria
Alcaudique
Celín

Collado
Beneji
Dalías

llanos
El Río Grande
El Río Chico
Casablanca

Cuesta Vieja
El Corral
A-347

laza
erra
Los López
Los Pérez
La Parra
AL-103
Pampanico
Santa María
del Águila

Los Moras
ches
La Alquería
El Pardo
Loma del Boque

Pompolos
La Fuente
del Ahijado
Tarambana

de Huarea
La Alcazaba
El Ejido
Las Norias
de Daza
La Mojonera

La Cueva
elo de la Juana
Guainos
Bajos
El Lance de
la Virgen
Adra
El Puente del Río
El Campillo
Balanegra
Matagorda
Chozas
San Agustín

Playa de Balerma
Balerma
AL-9036
Guardias
Viejas
Almarimar

MEDITERRÁNEO

11

A "cortijo" (farmhouse) in the Alpujarra.

Towards 2700 BC there appeared a new cultural centre, based on the wealth of mining at the easternmost end of the Alpujarra; the most important settlement is known as Los Millares, in the Gádor mountain-range. A new centre of culture arose in later centuries, this time to the west of the Alpujarra. It is the so-called Megalithic culture, with its centre in Antequera and Huelva, and which later spread all over Europe. During this third millenium BC the Alpujarra, enclosed amid unscalable mountains, was slower in its development.

The Bronze Age in Spain also began in the Alpujarra. The Argar culture began in Almería, which was later to spread to a large part of Europe between 1700 and 1400 BC. It was during this millenium too that in Western Andalusia the rich and powerful state of Tartessos arose, concerning whose history there are still substantial lacunae.

In the first millenium BC colonisation by people from the east began: Greeks, Phoenicians, Carthaginians, and the Celts came from the north. This period comes to a head with Roman colonisation. None of these peoples were to leave a particulary lasting mark on the area, perhaps the most visible marks are those left by the Romans on the coast (Almuñécar, where there are important remains of an aqueduct and the columbarium).

In 711, with the advent of the Arabs, historical information concerning the region began to become available. There are stories existing concerning the local people which describe them as independent warriors and with a certain penchant for banditry.

In the 10th century there was a rebellion in south Andalusia against the creation of the caliphate of Cordoba, headed by Omar ben Hafsun. The people of the Alpujarra took sides with those vying for independence, and so Abd ar-Rahman III himself had to cross the Sierra Nevada to Ugíjar and, after several days' siege, took the castle of Juviles near Cádiar.

During the times of the petty kingdoms or *taifas* (11th century on) the *taifa* of Almería came to the forefront thanks to its silk industry. The Alpujarra became a silk-producing centre, and this period also produced two writers of note in the area: Ibn Sharaf and Ibn Omar. In the 13th century Moslem sway was restricted to the Nazrid kingdom of Granada. The Granada administrators divided the Alpujarra into 'tahas' (large municipal areas), building castles in each of the

areas. The silk industry flourished during this period too.

From 1487 onwards the Christian grip on the Kingdom of Granada (roughly the present-day provinces of Granada, Málaga and Almería) tightened, a situation which was aggravated by the dynastic problems between Mulei Hacen, El Zagal and Boabdil. Between 1487 and 1488 the western and eastern parts of the kingdom fell. The latter part was in the hands of El Zagal, and was exchanged against a lifelong domain in the Alpujarra for this rival of Mulei Hacen and Boabdil. However, shortly afterwards he was expelled to Africa, where he was incarcerated.

On 2nd January 1492 Granada capitulated and Boabdil signed the declaration of surrender. He too was granted a domain in the Alpujarra, with residence on the banks of

Donkeys of Alpujarra.

Countryside around Lecrín.

Countryside.

The Alpujarra's splendid fruit.

the Andarax (near Ugíjar), but, like his uncle, he was forced to leave for Africa, which he did in October 1493, becoming established in Fez. During preparations for this trip his wife Moraima died, and she is believed to be buried in the castle of the Lecrín Valley. By virtue of the Declaration of Surrender of 1492, the Catholic Monarchs granted the Moslem population respect for their creed, uses and customs, as well as their property; this notwithstanding, the sharing out of land amongst the Castilian aristrocracy, added to the heavy-handed policies of Cardinal Cisneros, led to unrest and open rebellion, the most serious episode being that of 1500 in the Alpujarra, which was put down only with great difficulty.

Things improved with the advent of Charles V to the throne. However, under Philip II heavy-handedness was again the name of the game; this monarch's policies led to the decree of 1567 whereby the use of Arabic, together with the holding of Morisco beliefs and the practise of Morisco customs, were all banned.

Towards the end of 1568 the Morisco rebel leaders agreed on a general uprising, but the failure of the same in the Granada meant that the brunt of the rebellion was borne in the Alpujarra. The rebels controlled various ports via which they received help from North Africa. In the Lecrín Valley, on 27th December 1568, Aben Humeya was proclaimed king. The solemn coronation was held a few days later in Cádiar, in an olive-grove. Aben Humeya, otherwise known as Aben Omeya, came from an old Moslem family related to the Omeya family. His people had

Trévelez and the surrounding area.

become converted to Christianity, and so he bore the name of Fernando de Córdoba y Válor; when the rebellion began he changed his name.

Still in December 1568 the Moriscos made their stronghold in the Lecrín Valley, repulsing the Christian troops under the command of the marquis of Mondéjar, until eventually the latter crossed the Tablate Bridge and entered the Alpujarra. In the meantime, Aben Farag, Aben Humeya's lieutenant, had made incursions into Lanjarón and other parts of the Western Alpujarra such as Orgiva. Between 10th and 18th January, the Christian troops gradually reduced the *tahas* of Poqueira, Pitres, Juviles and Ugíjar.

Aben Humeya preferred guerrilla warfare, and once more marched off to the west, going up the Lecrín Valley and crossing the Tablate Bridge once more, thus cutting the communication lines of the Christians. At this point the marquis of Vélez came into the fray with reserve troops in the east. The marquis of Mondéjar passed over once more to the western part, but the Moriscos held up his advance at the Guájares Rock (on the way to Salobreña), and so the Moriscos yet again entered the Alpujarra.

Aben Humeya, hiding in the areas of Bérchules, Válor and Mecina-Bombarón, was surprised in an ambush in the latter locality, the place of residence of Aben Aboo, cousin and later successor to the Morisco rebel leader. During the first months of 1569 atrocities were committed on both sides, such as the 800 dead in Válor. In April command of the Christian troops was taken by John of Austria, brother of Philip II. In May

Olive-groves of the Alpujarra.   *Detail of Pórtugos.* ▷

the insurrection opened up and reached Axarquía, the Bentomiz mountain-range, Baza and Eastern Almería, although in June the last Málaga Moriscos were defeated in Frigiliana. Between June and July, Christian troops were victorious in the Eastern Alpujarra (Berja and Ugíjar), but in August the Morisco troops once more took Padul and other localities in the Lecrín Valley. The marquis of Mondéjar was relieved of his command by John of Austria.

In October 1569 a conspiration against Aben Humeya was hatched in Cádiar. The underlying motifs were varied in nature: there was the ambition of Aben Aboo, the confrontation between Aben Humeya and the Turkish troops, the hatred of his wife's family (since the Morisco king had killed several members of her family); there was even an element of jealousy. Aben Humeya was resting in Laujar de Andarax (to the east of Ugíjar). He was assassinated by his cousin, who succeeded him. He was buried there, but when the fighting ended, John of Austria had his remains taken to Guadix. The second Morisco king began his reign well by a victory over the Christians in Orgiva, but when the brother of Philip II came into the fray, he was forced back to the heights of the mountains. At that time the Moriscos of Granada and La Vega had already been expelled into other provinces. By 1570 the Morisco rebel leader had only 300 men under him. Finally he too was assassinated and his remains taken to Granada.

With the putting down of the rebellion the surviving Moriscos, estimated to be some 80,000, were expelled to Western Andalu-

Typical corner.

Typical street in Pampaneira ▷

sia, La Mancha and Castile. A few thousand of them managed to hold on until the general expulsion of the Moriscos from the country, an event which happened in 1610 during the reign of Philip III. A large part of the territory of Granada was devastated. The new settlers came from Galicia, León, Asturias and Castile – all told 12,542 families who settled in 270 localities, leaving another 130 places abandoned for ever. From these times on the district suffered a general decline and sunk into historical oblivion; the only event worthy of mention is its participation in the Spanish Civil War. After the uprising of 18th July 1936, the Granada, Almería and Málaga coast, as well as the central and eastern parts of the Alpujarra, were still in the hands of the government of the Spanish Republic. The rebels

had taken control of the capital, Granada, and did not venture any further than Lanjarón. Orgiva was evacuated and remained a sort of no-man's land until the end of the war. Wealthy families fled to the capital, and in the district atrocities were committed on both sides, more because of personal squabbles than for true political motives.

The post-Spanish Civil War period was one of hunger, aggravated by droughts until 1950. This situation was to be of benefit for the Alpujarra, since water was one thing which never lacked there.

And so we come to the end of the history of the Alpujarra. Today the area is thriving thanks to the growth of tourism, attracted to these parts by its various charms which make both a visit and permanent residence here a very pleasant thing.

Alpujarra countryside.

Alpujarra flora. ▷

THE TRIP

1. THE LECRÍN VALLEY

Though the trip proper begins in Orgiva, in this valley there are townships and places of historical importance, which make it easier to understand the past of the Alpujarra.

The Lecrín Valley lies between the Sierra Nevada and the Sierra Almijara; its name means "happy valley".

During the Morisco uprising, it was fought over tooth and nail by the Christians and Moriscos. Because of this fact the inhabitants were to suffer a great deal during the conflict. In this valley there are important localities such as Padul, Dúrcal and Lecrín.

The climate in this valley is varied, but there are no abrupt changes in temperatures as in the interior of the Alpujarra.

This means that currently, due to the fertility of the land and the weather, farming production is both varied and substantial.

The Lecrín Valley is bordered on the west by the Sierra Nevada, and is transversed by an important access route to the capital of the province which in turn serves as entry point from the west into the Alpujarra.

Overall view of Padul.

The countryside and part of Padul. ▷

Padul

Population: 7,000
Height above sea level: 750 m
Padul is located at the northern of the Lecrín Valley, some 6 km from Suspiro del Moro and 20 km from Granada along the N 323 highway.

From the Puerto del Suspiro del Moro (literally 'The Pass of the Moor's Sigh', standing 865 m above sea level) may be had the last splendid view of the city of Granada before descending the Lecrín Valley. The Moor in the pass's name is Boabdil, who, together with his mother, is said to have cried on this spot at the loss of his beloved Granada with the 1492 Capitulation imposed by the Catholic Monarchs. Legend also has it that Boabdil's mother retorted "Weep then like a woman over that you could not defend like a man". In all likelihood Boabdil did not know how to defend his city, since he was an inefficient governor and devoted his time to family squabbles, even going to the point of betraying his country.

In this town stands the 18th-century Palace of the Counts of Padul a 14th-century Arab fortified tower, and a 16th-century Renaissance parish church.

During the Morisco uprising the town was depopulated and devasted by the Moriscos in the wake of their victory in battle over the Christians, since it was an important access route to the Alpujarra.

Dúrcal: view of the Plaza de España.

The river Dúrcal and the fountain in the Plaza de España. ▷

Dúrcal

Population: 5,000
Height above sea level: 800 m
Eight km south from Padul, after crossing the river bearing the same name (and which is a tributary of the Guadalfeo) we come to Dúrcal itself.
This village is a combination of modern and traditional local architecture. The large Plaza de España, together with the parish church and the town hall, form its hub. Near this important village are the other localities of Cozvijar, Barrio Marchena, Cónchar, Nigueles and Acequias.
Only a few kilometres from Dúrcal one of the most hotly-fought episodes of the struggles between Christians and Moriscos occurred. In 1569 Nacoz, the Morisco rebel leader, ambushed a convoy of provisions going towards Orgiva, putting all the Christians in it to the sword.

Overall view of Lecrín.

View of Lecrín castle and part of the olive-groves. ▷

Lecrín

Population: 1, 500
Height above sea level: 700 m
This spot, also known as Talará, is some 6 km from Dúrcal.
Here are to be found the ruins of the castle raised by Mulei Hacen, the last king but one of Granada. In the cemetery ("rauda") the kings of Granada were buried; it is generally thought that the last burial was that of Moraima, the wife of Boabdil, the last monarch of the Nazrid kingdom. It is also thought that king Mulei Hacen himself was buried by his wife on the heights of the Mulhacén, which bears his name.

In Béznar, a few kilometres from Lecrín, Aben Humeya was was chosen king of the rebel Moriscos, althought the coronation itself did not take place until later in Cádiar.

The Lecrín festivities are held on the 8th December, in honour of the Immaculate Conception.

Tablate bridge.

Tablate: the hermitage of Our Lady of the Sorrows and the New Bridge. ▷

2. THE TABLATE BRIDGE

This is a place of great historical importance, since it is the true western access point to the Alpujarra.

It lies 6 km from Lecrín. Nearby stands the Hermitage of Our Lady of the Sorrows. Here too the old Inn of the Sorrows stands, where in 1872 Pedro Antonio de Alarcón stayed, as do many present-day visitors before embarking on their trips around the region.

It was once a place of great strategic importance. On 10th January 1569 one of the first battles between Christians and Moriscos was fought here, after the uprising of the latter. The Christians, under the command of the marquis of Mondéjar, mahaged to cross the Tablate Bridge which led to the heart of the Alpujarra. Later, at another moment in the struggle, the Moriscos managed to dominate it as well as the Lecrín Valley itself.

Overall view of Lanjarón.

Lanjarón's Arab castle. ▷

3. LANJARÓN

Population: 4,500
Height above sea level: 725 m
Seven kilometres from the Tablate Bridge along our itinerary, we come to Lanjarón, of which Gerald Brenan once said that it "stretches like a balustrade all along a sloped escarpment".

Lanjarón is famous for its medicinal waters and its spa, one of the most visited and busiest in the whole of Spain, which was already nationally famous in the 19th century. Hence, this spot can boast many hotels of different categories offering abundant accommodation, much more than any other town in the Alpujarra; as a result it is a fre-

quent stopping off place for the area's travellers.

The parish church is 16th century. There are also remains of an Arab castle built on an almost inaccessible hill. The town's past has two important moments: on 8th March 1500, the Arab population inside the castle withstood the onslaught of Ferdinand the Catholic, who had come armed with artillery.

Three hundred Moslems died, among them their black chief, who killed himself by throwing himself off a tall tower. The people of Lanjarón, shut in inside the mosque, were practically all killed when it was blown up.

The second moment of historical impor-

Two views of Lanjarón's spa.

tance came on 28th December 1568, one day after the proclamation of Aben Humeya as head of the rebel Moriscos. The Senior Sheriff, Aben Farag, during a campaign throughout the Alpujarra in order to incite people to rebellion, burned Lanjarón church, together with some 20 Christians inside.

The festivities of Lanjarón are held on the following dates: the patron saint's day (St. Sebastian) is 20th January; on 24th June the "water and ham" festivities are held, and the 7th October the festivites of the Virgin of the Rosary.

Typical street of Lanjarón. ▷

Three views of Lanjarón.

View of Orgiva.

4. ORGIVA

Population: 6,500

Height above sea level: 450 m

Nine km from Lanjarón, along the route suggested in this book, we come to Orgiva, the true capital of Western Alpujarra. It is the judicial district of the entire area we are visiting, as well as being the largest commercial and trading centre in the region, hence making this town a mixture of both modern and traditional aspects. It is an intersection and the way to the centre of the Alpujarra.

For this reason Orgiva has been regarded as the most important locality on this itinerary, and this is where the visit proper really starts. As can be seen on a map, four roads lead out of Orgiva. One goes to Tor-

viscón, thence to East Alpujarra and the Granada coast via La Rábita. Another leads to Vélez de Benaudalla, towards Salobreña and the Costa del Sol.

A third road leads to Granada via Lanjarón and the Lecrín Valley.

Finally the fourth (the one chosen as our route) ascends to Pampaneira, Trevélez, Ugíjar and the other places mentioned later on.

All these factors have meant that hotel capacity is large in Orgiva; in addition it also has numerous bars and places of entertainment like discotheques.

Noteworthy monuments here are the 16th-century parish church with its mixture of Baroque and Renaissance; the Palace of the Counts of Sástago; the remains of a Nazrid fortified Arab tower; the very dete-

Orgiva: the hermitage of St. Sebastian.

riorated remains of a 15th-century Arab oil mill, the Molinos de Benizalte.

The most important historical event of this town happened after the episode in Lanjarón at the beginning of 1569. The troops of Aben Farag were marching towards Orgiva, where the mayor, one Sarabia, had shut himself inside a fortified tower with Morisco hostages to await the arrival of the marquis of Mondéjar, who came in time to relieve the besieged.

On the Friday before Good Friday are held the festivities of the Christ of Expiration. Between the 29th September and 2nd October there are various fairs and festivities.

Orgiva: parish Church.

A typical Alpujarra kitchen. ▷

View of the river Chico at Carataunas.

The Barranco (Ravine) del Poqueira.

5. ON THE WAY TO THE POQUEIRA RAVINE

During the 14-km climb up from Orgiva to Pampaneira, we shall come across roads leading off to three typical Alpujarra villages. The first road leads off the Cáñar, a village of some 1,000 inhabitants standing at more than 1,000 metres above sea level, some 8 km from Orgiva.

Almost at the foot of this road we are on, we shall find the village of Carataunas, some 7 km from Orgiva, which is still relatively unspoilt, and shows few signs of the tourist boom. Finally we see Soportújar, 8 km from Orgiva. Almost the whole of the municipal district lies within the Sierra Nevada National Park. In this same area, near the Sortes Cave, in the homestead of a friend, Federico García Lorca once stayed while writing "La Casada Infiel" (The Unfaithful wife), according to Rafael Gómez Montero.

6. THE POQUEIRA RAVINE

After leading these diversions behind we are already in the Poqueira Ravine, a very impressive part of the country whose terraced walls rise up to the Veleta. The vegetation here is lush and abundant, with different colours and a raging river, the Poqueira, in the background.

However, most worthy of note here are the three villages perched on the sides: Pampaneira, Bubión and Capileira, three white spots which compete with the perpetual snows of the Veleta.

It is these three villages that have most benefitted from the tourist boom over the past few years; paradoxically they were never visited by either of the bestknown travellers of these parts, Alarcón and Brenan. However, today's traveller has chosen them as centres for journeying and even as places of residence.

Overall view of Pampaneira.

Picturesque corner of Pampaneira.

7. PAMPANEIRA

The first village we come to in the Poqueira Ravine is Pampaneira, some 14 km from Orgiva.

It has a 16th-century Baroque parish church, with an interesting reredos and Mudejar coffering. It is on the Historical Villages list. In 1976 is was awarded the provincial prize for the Most Attractive Village, and in 1977 and 1978 the National Tourism Prize for Best-Kept Spanish Village.

The village is active in tourist initiatives. It has good hotel capacity, offered by a variety of hostels, hotels and private accommodation. It is easy to find restaurants and bars where the gastronomic delights of the region may be savoured. There are also many shops selling pottery, cloths and other examples of Alpujarra crafts in general. Houses here, like those elsewhere in the Poqueira Ravine, are made of stone with flat slate roofs ("terraos") on which it is possible to walk. The Pampaneira flowerpots or "tinaos" are very impressive in their profusion of flowers. At the same time, walks through the various streets are a great attraction: the streets of Silencio, del Cristo, Federico García Lorca, or the Plaza de la Libertad, where the parish church stands.

Also important are the numerous fountains to be found here; some of the most noteworthy are the following: the Fuente (fountain) de los Poetas, the Chumpaneira, the

Overall view of Pampaneira.

Pampaneira: the "Chumpaneira" fountain and two typical corners. ▷

Fuente Agrilla de Sonsoles, the Fuente del Caudillo and the Fuente del Cerrillo.

The name of Pampaneira, though suggested as being Galician in origin, is really Latin. It means "producer of vine tendrils", thus associating it closely with the production of vineyards.

Currently Pampaneira, together with Bubión and Capileira, are the favourite localities for tourists both from home and abroad.

Due to changing weather conditions during the summer and winter months visitors come in a steady stream throughout the year. Stays in the area range from a weekend, to a longer period, and even permanent residence as happens in a good many cases.

Apart from the attractions inherent in this place, which have made it worldfamous, we should add some other curious facts. One of these is the birth, in the Poqueira Ravine, of the child who is destined to be the next Dalai Lama in Tibet, whose journey to be confirmed in this destiny launched the Alpujarra to world fame.

Between 3rd and 5th May are held the festivities in honour of the Holy Cross, culminating with the "Burial of the Vixen". Also well-known are the pig-killing festivities, held between 5th and 8th December.

FUENTE DE SAN ANTONIO=
=HUMPANEIRA=

No digas nunca de este agua no beberé
pues esta fuente que aquí ves
es fuente de la virtud
y tiene tal magnitud
que a beber su agua invita
la confirmó un devoto
que feligrés fué de esta Iglesia.
Y soltero que la bebe con intención de casarse
¡no falla!, pues al instante......
novia tiene ¡ya lo ves!

Picturesque corner of Pampaneira.

Overall view of Bubión.

8. BUBIÓN

Population: 600
Height above sea level: 1,300 m
Two kilometres out of Pampaneira there comes a fork in the road. To the left, the road leads us up to Bubión, standing two kilometres after the fork. Bubión is equidistant between the other two villages of the Poqueira Ravine. It is also on the Historical Villages list. The parish church is 16th century. Next to it there are the remains of a Nazrid Arab fortified tower. Also of interest is a visit to the Hermitage of St. Anthony. The Andalusian regional government has built a hotel complex within this municipal area, near the old, no longer standing village of Alguastar. The complex is known as the "Poqueira Tourist Complex", and the running of it has been entrusted to a cooperative. Hotel capacity is large, and hiking, horsetrekking, or all-purpose vehicle trips are organised.

In addition to the hotel beds, Bubión has more space to offer within the old part of the village. It also has numerous typical bars, restaurants and workshops producing articles of Alpujarra craftsmanship and precious metalwork.

The name of Bubión also comes from Latin and means "land of oxen".

The festivities of Bubión are held round about 20th January in honour of St. Sebastian. On the last Sunday but one in August are organised the festivities of Christians versus Moors.

Bubión: detail and partial view.

Part of Capileira.

9. CAPILEIRA

Population: 900

Height above sea level: 1,436 m

By carrying on along this rising road we come to Capileira. This village, yet again on the Historical Villages list, stands at the head (hence its name, possible from the Latin meaning 'head of hair') of the Poqueira Ravine, facing the Veleta. Of the three villages in the ravine this is the most popular with the tourists, and therefore it has a great deal of accommodation, and a great many bars, restaurants and artisan workshops. The lower part of the village, standing over the Tajo del Diablo (Devil's Cut) has commanding sweeping views, and is a must on the traveller's itinerary. Going down towards this lower part of the village from the road, we shall pass through the streets of Dr. Castillo, the Calvario square, the alley of la Campana, the Panteón Viejo square or the Cuesta Iglesia street, where the parish church stands.

On the Calvario square stands a sculpture depicting a Guisando bull, and is a gift from the Diputación of Avila. Recently a Culture Centre was built, named after Pedro Antonio de Alarcón; it is a typical Alpujarra house, as well as being a museum and residence for artists. Its name of course is that of the famous Guadix traveller, even though he did not pass through Capileira on his journeys. From Capileira a road leads off to the Vele-

49

Capileira: detail and overall view.

ta peak, after passing through the Prado Llano. Thence it leads on to Granada via the Sierra Nevada Ski resort. It is best to make the trip during the summer months in vehicles properly equipped for high mountain driving.

There are also important fountains in this village, some of the most noteworthy being that of El Cerezo, El Calvario and that of Almúñar.

Local festivities are held on the last Sunday in April, in honour of the Virgin of the Head, a polychrome statue which was a gift from the Catholic Monarchs. On 5th August a *romería* or pilgrimage to the Veleta Deak is organised.

Two views of Capileira and Mount Veleta. ▷

Overall view of Pitres.

Two views of Pitres. ▷

10. PITRES

Population: 800
Height above sea level: 1,295 m
From Capileira one returns along the same road leading to the diversion at the exit point from Pampaneira. From this spot it is 4 km to Pitres. Along this road we travel through the Blood Ravine, which separates the *taha* of Poqueira from that of Pitres.

Due to its strategic situation, this place was the scene of an important battle during the Morisco uprising, which ended with the victory of the troops of the marquis of Mondéjar.

It was here too that the fighting front between both sides in the Spanish Civil War remained practically unaltered for the duration of that conflict.

Just before reaching Pitres there is a road leading off to Mecina-Fondales and the 1st class campsite called "El Balcón de Pitres", with its restaurant and swimming-pool open all the year round.

Pitres is also known as La Taha, since it was the main village of the old Arab *taha*. Of note in Pitres is the spacious square where the majestically white parish church stands. There are also bars and restaurants in this square.

Festivities are held on St. Roque's day (16th August); on the 12th of the same month a *romería* or pilgrimage is organised.

Overall view and a typical street in Pórtugos.

11. PÓRTUGOS

Population: 500
Height above sea level: 1,300 m
Two km from Pitres, after crossing the river Bermejo and leaving the roads to Capilerilla, Atalbéitar and Ferreirola, one reaches Pórtugos. The most noteworthy spot in this place is just outside the village. This is the "Fuente Agria" (Sour Spring), a fountain with ferruginous waters which give the river bed along which they run a reddish tinge. Nearby is found "El Chorreón", a delightful spot with reddish waterfalls. Between both stands the Hermitage of Our Lady of the Sorrows.
Festivities are held on 8th October (Virgin of the Rosary). There is also a fair in the village between the 17th and 19th of the same month.

Square and fountain, the "Fuente Agria" and Hermitage of Our Lady of the Sorrows.

FUENTE AGRIA

Views of Busquístar.

12. BUSQUÍSTAR

Population: 700
Height above sea level: 1,160 m
Along the two kilometres between Pórtugos and Busquístar one travels through one of the largest chestnut-tree woods in the area.

Busquístar is a small village, all of it covered with "launa" or slate, it is possibly the village where most roofs of this material are to be found together.

Outside the village, on a rock, there are the remains of an Arab mosque whence there is a fine panoramic view of nearby villages.

Festivities are held here in honour of St. Philip and St. James, accompanied by the Virgin of Pains, on 3rd and 4th May.

Trevélez: overall view.

Two views of Trevélez. ▷

13. TREVÉLEZ

Population: 1,150
Height above sea level: 1,476 m
After crossing the ravines of El Tesoro, Los Alisos and La Bina, during a 9-km climb, one reaches the village of Trevélez, the highest village in Spain. Its parish church dates from the 16th century.
The locality comprises three districts (hence its name of "tre(s) vélez") – upper, middle and lower – standing at the foot of the Mulhacén as Capileira does the Veleta.

The village crosses the river Trevélez (a trout river, and tributary of the Guadalfeo).
Local cured hams are world famous: they are dried in the wind of the mountain, and may be easily acquired in the locality. There are numerous bars and restaurants which serve it as appetiser; again there is abundant accommodation. Here too is to be found the "Camping Trevélez" campsite.
Festivities are held on St. Anthony's day (13th June); the *romería* or pilgrimage to the Mulhacén is held on the 5th August, in honour of the Virgin of the Snows.

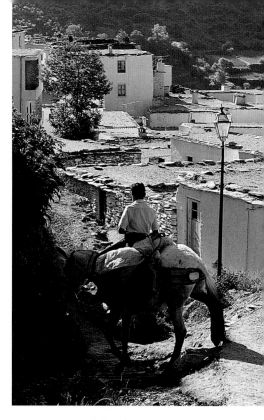

Three views of Trévelez.

The river Trevélez, waterfall and the area near.

Part of Juviles.

14. JUVILES

Population: 500
Height above sea level: 1,260 m
Along the 12-kilometre drop from Trevélez to Juviles, we shall always find before us the most impressive walls of the Contraviesa mountainrange, a rival to the Sierra Nevada.

Just before reaching the village there is a road leading off to Cástaras, where the Conjuro mines are to be found. Following this road one links in to the final part of our trip, at Torviscón.

Juviles is a small whitewashed village with an interesting stone-coloured parish church surrounded by gardens. The village has bars and accommodation.

Juviles was the scene for two historic events, the first of which goes back to the 10th century. In order to crush the revolt led by Omar Ben Hafsun, Abd ar-Rahman III took the castle of Juviles. During the Morisco uprising, the chroniclers have recorded the atrocities committed by the Christian armies against the Morisco populace.

Festivities are held on 20th January (St. Sebastian) and on 20th October (Virgin of the Rosary).

15. BÉRCHULES

Population: 2,000
Height above sea level: 1,320 m
This village is located 6 km after Juviles, half a kilometre off the road. Terraced farming and chestnuts are still predominant features in this area. Through this part too run the rivers Chico and Grande of the Bérchules, both of which are trout rivers and tributaries of the Guadalfeo. It has ferruginous water springs. It is famous for its fruit, wine and cured ham. The mountains to the north of Bérchules were chosen by Aben Humeya as a daytime refuge, since the military tactics used by the Morisco troops was guerilla warfare.
Festivities are held on 25-26th April (St. Mark) and on 27th July the *romería* or pilgrimage of St. Pantaleon is organised.

Bérchules: parish church and a typical corner.

16. MECINA BOMBARÓN

Population: 1,300
Height above sea level: 1,200 m
Equidistant (4 km) from Bérchules and Mecina-Bombarón there is a road leading off to Cádiar, a village which we shall visit when this trip gradually turns towards Orgiva. Of Mecina-Bombarón Gerald Brenan said: "This is a large village, partially white-washed and with many large houses scattered amongst chestnut woods". Aben Aboo, made his residence in one of these houses; later his cousin Aben Humeya assassinated and succeeded him in his command over the Morisco troops. This village was also chosen by Aben Humeya as a nighttime den after taking refuge in the mountains.

Mecina Bombarón: overall view and the Old Bridge.

Part of Yegen.

At the exit point of this locality one crosses the river Mecina, a tributary of the river Adra. Only a few metres from the road, there is a well-preserved Arab bridge over it.

Festivities are held on 15th May (St. Isidore), and 29-30th September (St. Michael and the Virgin of Ransoms).

17. YEGEN

Population: 750

Height above sea level: 1,000 m

Some 4 km from Mecina-Bombarón we come across the village immortalised by the writer Gerald Brenan. Yegen is internationally famous since it was the home and main subject matter of this writer's book entitled "South from Granada". In this work, the British hispanist goes into an anthropological, cultural, historical and geographical study of the Alpujarra, but taking Yegen, its inhabitants and customs, as the centre-piece. A small plaque indicates the house where Gerald Brenan once lived. A half-century before, Pedro Antonio de Alarcón said of this village that it was "a bunch of flowers and fragrant herbs placed there by a lover in the lap of the white Solair" (Sierra Nevada). The mountains protect the village from the north wind. There are abundant walnut trees, chestnuts and oaks.

Festivities are held on 1-2nd January (the God Child and the Name of Jesus).

Yegen: plaque on the house of Gerald Brenan, square and church.

VALOR

Gastronomía morisca

Patria de Aben Humeya

Festejos de Moros y Cristianos

Mensa Alpujarreña

Announcement lauding the virtues of Válor.

18. VÁLOR

Population: 2,000
Height above sea level: 900 m
A 6 km from Yegen lies the village of Válor, located between to very deep ravines, in a sort of peaceful mountain backwater. It could well be said that we are approaching the Gádor mountain range.

Valor is a place of great historic importance since it was the birthplace of Aben Humeya in 1520. He belonged to an old family related to the Omeya, but after the Christian conquest of the kingdom of Granada the family was converted, to Christianity, and so his original name had been Fernando de Válor. With the onset of the Morisco uprising, he changed to his betterknown name, and led the revolt.

In the first months of 1569 the Morisco population of Válor rebelled against the "Christian damages and outrages" and defeated 800 men.

On the way out of Válor there is a diversion at Mecina-Alfahara, leading to Mairena and Laroles, which eventually goes on to Guadix after passing through La Ragua mountain pass.

The festivities of Christians versus Moriscos are well worth seeing. They are held in honour of the Holy Christ of the Ivy, on 14-15th September.

*Two views of
Válor.*

Mecina Alfahara:
overall view and
detail.

Santuary of Our Lady of Martyrdom at Ugíjar.

19. UGÍJAR

Population: 3,000
Height above sea level: 560 m
After crossing the river Nechite (6 km from Válor) we come to the easternmost part of our trip – Ugíjar. This is the metropolis and the most important commercial centre of the Eastern Alpujarra. Ugíjar is a crossroads leading to Láujar de Andarax, Berja Murtas or Cádiar (the route we are to travel on eventually). On entering the small town one is confronted with the impressive red rocks which act as a natural wall. The 16th-century Sanctuary of Our Lady of the Martyrdom (patron saint of the Alpujarra) is of interest. This statue is the object of an important cult rendered by local coastal fishermen. Outside the locality stands the Hermitage of St. Anton. The spot has substantial accommodation, and a wealth of bars, shops and restaurants.

According to Gerald Brenan, Strabo once said that this village possessed a temple dedicated to Athena and was visited by Ulysses, attracted to the gold which could be extracted from its rivers. For this reason, in 1929 a French company intended to build an artificial lake to make it easier to extract.

During the 1569 Morisco uprising Aben Aboo had more than 200 Christians put to the sword at the beginning of the struggle.

In 1888 a silk factory was set up, a reminder of the old boom during the times of the Nazrids and the Moriscos. Festivities are held between the 10th and 14th October, in honour of the Virgin of the Martyrdom.

*Ugíjar: the Arch
Fountain and
gardens.*

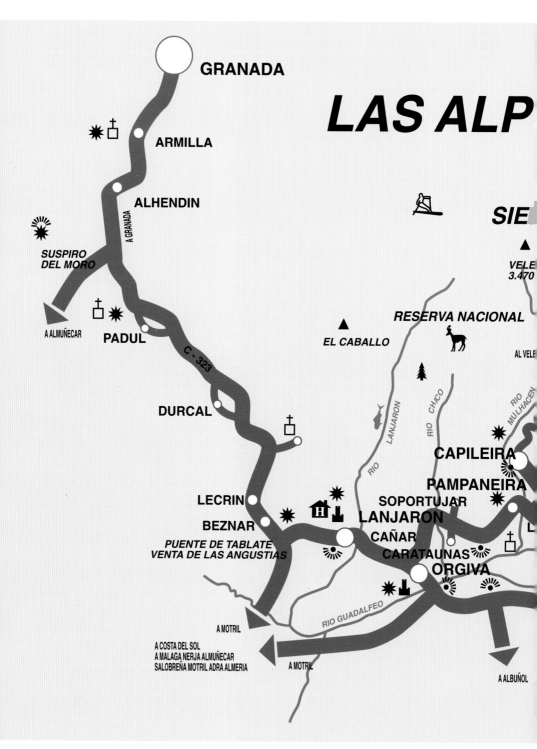

GRANADA

LAS ALP

ARMILLA

ALHENDIN

A GRANADA

SUSPIRO
DEL MORO

SIE

VELE
3.470

A ALMUÑECAR

PADUL

C - 323

RESERVA NACIONAL

EL CABALLO

AL VELE

DURCAL

RIO LANJARON

RIO CHICO

RIO MULHACEN

RIO

CAPILEIRA

PAMPANEIRA

LECRIN

SOPORTUJAR

BEZNAR

LANJARON

CAÑAR

PUENTE DE TABLATE
VENTA DE LAS ANGUSTIAS

CARATAUNAS

L

ORGIVA

A MOTRIL

RIO GUADALFEO

A COSTA DEL SOL
A MALAGA NERJA ALMUÑECAR
SALOBREÑA MOTRIL ADRA ALMERIA

A MOTRIL

A ALBUÑOL

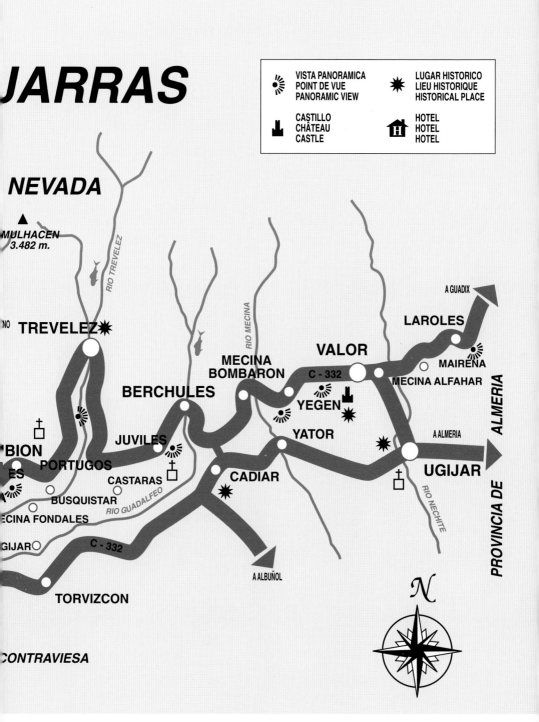

JARRAS

VISTA PANORAMICA
POINT DE VUE
PANORAMIC VIEW

LUGAR HISTORICO
LIEU HISTORIQUE
HISTORICAL PLACE

CAȘTILLO
CHÂTEAU
CASTLE

HOTEL
HOTEL
HOTEL

NEVADA

▲
MULHACEN
3.482 m.

RIO TREVELEZ

RIO MECINA

A GUADIX

NO TREVELEZ

LAROLES

MAIRENA

VALOR

MECINA ALFAHAR

MECINA
BOMBARON

C - 332

BERCHULES

YEGEN

ALMERIA

JUVILES

YATOR

A ALMERIA

BION

PORTUGOS

ES

CASTARAS

CADIAR

UGIJAR

BUSQUISTAR

RIO GUADALFEO

ECINA FONDALES

PROVINCIA DE

GIJAR

C - 332

RIO NECHITE

A ALBUÑOL

TORVIZCON

N

CONTRAVIESA

73

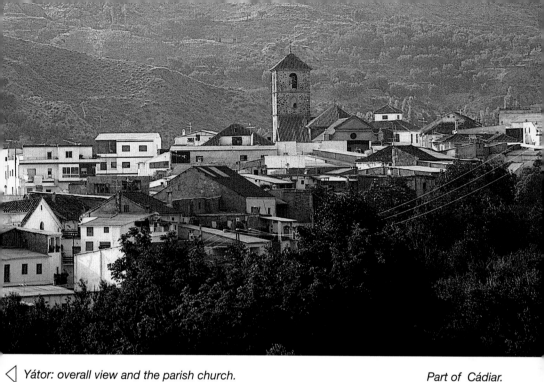

◁ *Yátor: overall view and the parish church.*

Part of Cádiar.

20. CÁDIAR

Population: 2,500
Height above sea level: 700 m
Six km from Ugíjar one leaves the road to Murtas, Albuñol and La Rábita, taking another leading off to Cádiar. After 7 km along a deserted road one reaches the small town of Yátor with its stone church-fortress whose square tower has on each face of the bell tower two half-point arches decorated with mosaics. This small town is traversed by the same river Mecina we have mentioned before.

Six km from Yátor stands Cádiar, after taking a diversion from the road which took us on the upper part of our trip. Cádiar is an important town, near which the source and early stages of the river Guadalfeo are to be found. In the opinion of Gerald Brenan, Cádiar is the centre point or heart of the Alpujarra.

The 16th-century Renaissance stone parish church stands in a large square, and combines traditional Alpujarra building techniques with more modern ones. It is reached along the streets called St. Isidro and Real. Cádiar is a commercial centre with good accommodation, restaurants, bars and shops.

The town's main claim to historical fame is that me olive-grove when Aben Humeya was crowned lies near the old part of the town; this part is therefore the setting for the well-known play by Martínez de la Rosa. It was in Cádiar too that the conspiration against Aben Humeya was hatched and executed. It was also the homeland of Aben Xaguar, the uncle of the Morisco rebel leader and his lieutenant. It was the occasional place of residence of the Morisco King.

Festivities are held on 3rd February (St. Blas) and 5-9th October, when instead of water the town fountains spout wine.

The fountain and Royal Street in Cádiar.

Part of Torviscón.

21. TORVISCÓN. THE END OF THE ITINERARY

Population: 2,500
Heigt above sea level: 684 m

The river Guadalfeo runs alongside the road for the 21 km separating Cádiar from Torviscón. From the road there are magnificent views of the Sierra Nevada to be had, with the most important peaks (Mulhacén, Veleta) be to seen. At the exit point from Cádiar there is a road leading off to the Granada coast of Albuñol, and then another to Juviles (via Cástaras) which has already been mentioned in our itinerary. Torviscón is located on the water course of the same name which bears its intermittent waters down to the Guadalfeo. The creamy colour of the house here matches that of the water course. The old capital of the Contraviesa could be regarded as "the favourite city of the sun" in the works of Pedro Antonio de Alarcón. Festivities are held on 17-18th January (St. Anton) and on 3-4th October fairs are held.

After Torviscón, the southernmost point of our journey, we follow the road leading us westward, ever in the company of the river Guadalfeo. Along these 20 km to Orgiva we first of all come to a turn-off which passes through Albuñol and continues on to the coastal Granada province resort of La Rábita, near the province of Almería. Then one passes by Tablones, and eventually we reach Orgiva, our starting point, chosen since it is the meeting point of various access roads to the heart of the region. It should not be forgotten that the route described in this guide is only one of the many possible ones. It has been chosen in terms of the tourist attractions of the towns and villages described, as well as its historical, geographical and cultural interest. There remain a great many places, above all in the eastern part of the Alpujarra, which the reader will no doubt discover for him or herself.

"Sacromonte omelette".

FOOD AND DRINK

The cuisine of the Alpularra has preserved all the traditional ingredients of Arab-Andalusian cooking, and embraces the two native gastronomic sources – Morisco and Christian.

There are many delicious typically Alpujarra dishes waiting to be tasted by any would-be gourmet. Perhaps the king of them all is the world famous mountain-air-cured Trevélez ham. Other forms of sausage are also to be noted (as well as black puddings).

Typical Alpujarra fare is rich in calories, adapted to the climate of the area, some of the typical dishes being: country dumplings, hotpot a la *gitanilla,* kid *a lo cortijero,* Alpujarra soup (with chopped almonds), paps *a lo pobre, sacromonte* and shepherds' omelette, oatmeal with peppers, beans with ham, en *orza* ham, Alpujarra trout, soused partridge, lamb and the Alpujarra dish containing ham, eggs and paps *a lo pobre.*

All this delicious fare can be washed down with good Alpujarra wines: wines from the coast, from the Contraviesa, Albuñol and Albondón.

Concerning confectionery, the Alpujarra has a wide variety of delicious cakes and dainties (again Arab-Andalusian in origin) such as Pampaneira doughnuts, Morisco sweets, candied egg yolks, *soplillos,* fritters with chocolate, liqueured cakes and other sorts of cakes.

The honey of the Alpujarra (as well as its jams) is also well-known.

The delicious desserts of the Alpujarra.

CONTENTS

EDITORIAL ESCUDO DE ORO, S.A.
I.S.B.N. 84-378-1614-9
Printed by FISA - Escudo de Oro, S.A.
Legal Dep. B. 48008-2002